All the Untils

All the Untils
poems for then and now

BY Lee Kiblinger

RESOURCE *Publications* • Eugene, Oregon

ALL THE UNTILS
Poems for Then and Now

Copyright © 2025 Lee Kiblinger. All rights reserved. Except for brief quotations in critical publications or reviews, no part of this book may be reproduced in any manner without prior written permission from the publisher. Write: Permissions, Wipf and Stock Publishers, 199 W. 8th Ave., Suite 3, Eugene, OR 97401.

Resource Publications
An Imprint of Wipf and Stock Publishers
199 W. 8th Ave., Suite 3
Eugene, OR 97401

www.wipfandstock.com

PAPERBACK ISBN: 979-8-3852-4638-0
HARDCOVER ISBN: 979-8-3852-4639-7
EBOOK ISBN: 979-8-3852-4640-3

VERSION NUMBER 04/16/25

To my family who has graced me
with hours and hours of love and laughter
that will echo beyond all untils . . .

He has made everything beautiful in its time.
Ecclesiastes 3:11 ESV

Contents

Acknowledgments | ix
Introduction | xi

Until

Untilled | 2
Underpainting | 3
Eves | 4
Prayers Before Faith | 5
Now and Then | 6
Marginals | 8
Months | 9
Raindrop Stories | 11
Aged | 13
A Memory | 15

Until Seeing

Pointillism | 18
It may not be an exodus, but what if . . . | 19
The Angel | 20
The Advent of Hindsight | 22
Next Year, Plant Roses | 24
Scenic Overlook | 26
New Moon | 28

Lake Day | 30
A Mast Year | 32
I try to learn jam band | 34
To Lose My Voice | 36
Thresholds | 37

Until Following

Dusted | 40
I share the shadow | 41
Lamenting Sackcloth | 43
Melting Point | 45
Leaving the Suburbs | 47
Dawnsongs | 49
Threadbare | 51
Edges | 53
Amen Is a Watershed | 55
A Box to Go with You | 57
Drafting | 58
Postlude | 60
Laughter Can Echo to Monday | 62
Matins | 63
Still Life | 64

Until Rising

Grandfather's Visit | 68
At the Park's Cancer Bell | 70
The Vanishing Point | 72
The Drift | 74
Windthrow | 76
Ms. Lela | 78
Espalier | 79
Unraveling | 81
A Final Volta | 82

Acknowledgments

A special thank you to the editors of the following for publishing these poems for the first time. I am forever grateful:

Agape Review
"Threshold"

Amethyst Review
"Now and Then"

Calla Press
"Aged"
"Grandfather's Visit"
"Laugher Can Echo to Monday"
"Melting Point"
"Prayers Before Faith"
"Scenic Overlook"

Clayjar Review
"Angel"
"Espalier"
"Lake Day"
"Months"
"Still Life"

Ekstasis Magazine
"Lamenting Sackcloth"
"Postlude"
"Underpainting"

The Habit Portfolio Substack
"Scenic Overlook"

Heart of Flesh Literary Journal
"Dawnsongs"
"Matins"
"Rain"

Rabbit Room Poetry Substack
"Edges"

Solid Food Press Anthology
"The Drift"
"I share the shadow"

Solum Press
"The Vanishing Point"

The Way Back to Ourselves
"A Mast Year"
"A New Moon"
"Raindrop Stories"

The Windhover
"Threadbare"

Thank you to my family and friends who have supported and encouraged me on this journey. When you wanted to laugh, you didn't. Thank you.

Another inadequate thank you to the gifted poets of The Habitation Poetry Group, a branch of The Habit Membership. The hours that you spend providing thoughtful feedback bless me richly, as does your friendship.

A special thank you to Lee Kohman and Joy Manning who love me well enough to hold my hand when I must toss the "darlings." Thank you to Megan Huwa who helped me tie this manuscript together. And thank you to Jesse Baker, my sounding board for the publishing process. I am so grateful to all of you.

Introduction

I think I'm younger than I am. When you spend hours in a classroom full of teenagers for so many years, they rub off on you: their interests, energies and even their naive snub at mortality. For better or worse, you find yourself living as if you were twenty instead of fifty. Most of my husband's patients are over seventy, so he comes home from work ready to discuss the puzzles to ward off dementia, the beauty of canes, or the best retirement plan, while I'm on the couch trying to figure out how to tag someone on Instagram.

So my recent foray into writing poetry still feels fitting, as though I've just graduated from college, and I'm finally finding myself. Yet I know that the following pages would not exist without the passage of time and all its intriguing mystery.

I, too, dreamt of being a writer in my teens, but never found myself a storyteller, so I let go of my own pen and stuck to teaching the glories of sentence construction and supporting details. (I think I can whip out a solid five-paragraph essay in about thirty minutes). But I always felt that only true "artists" could claim to be creative writers. Not minds that thrive on organization and checked boxes.

Until I wrote a poem.

One Sunday evening my husband and I were lamenting the approach of another Monday morning. The music of the postlude had passed, and we could only hear the sound of tomorrow's alarm clock and to-do list. In a single moment something in me wanted to capture the dread. Explain it. Rethink it. Make it universal. And a few minutes later, "Laughter can Echo to Monday" landed on the page.

Yes, this love for poetry seems a late discovery. It is. My children have grown, and I've entered the threshold of the empty nest. And in these quieter hours, I'm left to laugh with the Hand that held back this latent pleasure until now. What beautiful truth, when at age ninety, Czeslaw Milosz noted in his poem "Late Ripeness,"

Moments from yesterday and from centuries ago . . .
they dwell in us,
waiting for a fulfillment.

I've just been waiting. This collection of poems wasn't born until its time. And despite trying to act like I'm twenty, I have lived enough years to be humbled by the many untils scattered throughout the soil of my underground story. They have invited me to see life's canvas with fresh eyes. To look for hindsight and new moons. They've challenged me to leave the suburbs and follow my dust-covered Savior. And they've reminded me that one day I, too, will rise and run across an untrellised heaven.

So though I still beg my whys or whens or hows, I'm learning to find joy and rest in the wait.

And whether you live as if you're twenty or seventy, may you, too, discover *All the Untils* . . .

Until

Untilled

Mark 4:27

Our trowels hang from heavy belts
and we stoop to scoop
for untilled dirt,
some turn of root
to excavate hints
of a whispered *where,*
pilfer a glimpse of the soil's blueprint,
prepare for *now,* shovel the *when,*
spade plunged below,
grovel to our *know*
on mud-caked knees, bent
for *why*
this fate, this flood unleashing
the wail
against our *wait*—we're asked
to scatter seed
and sleep, uncurl our bodies
to the skies,
unbelt our burdens from time's waist—
for what is underground, we *know not how*
nor could imagine that en-earthed glory—
germination of buried story.

Underpainting

Wherever you come near the human race, there's layers and layers of nonsense. THORNTON WILDER

today is an underpainting—

in season's scumbling,
one more layer dries, opaque,

a visual humbling

until midnight blue
will shine cerulean

and the dull maroon
will only deepen

beneath the layers
of storied wait,

and firm brushstrokes
of a brighter day

spread the morrow's coat
with its holy glaze.

Eves

I see myself between
the Eves, having reached
for the same sweet skin
of knowing, only to swallow sour
all that grieves my within—
the shame of dis-covering
the good I believe
is out of reach unless
this rot is renamed
living—and mourning begins
my day before,
hope preserved
by flaming sword,
while I wait
in the darkened Eve—
for the coming of dawn
and the son-risen seed.

Prayers before Faith

Are prayers before faith phrases falling,
mist-like, evaporating to the ground—
waves of words echoed empty, hollow,
voiced but lost, just unheard sound?
Are cries crammed into cardboard boxes,
never opened in attics of dust—
pleas planted as seeds of what-ifs
in deserts windblown by sandy trust?
Do they move molecular, atoms combining
waiting for rising, concussive heat—
or hang like stars, with hope aligning
that forecast victory or herald defeat?
Do they come of age and ripen
like wild berries full of sweetened juice—
or are words wrapped up, cocoonlike,
until they warm, and then fly loose?

Their holding pattern is a mystery,
Still their wonder will incubate—
past utterance to future litany,
learned, rehearsed after timeless wait.

Now and Then

> *If things are real, then they are there all the time.*
> FROM C.S. LEWIS'S *The Lion, The Witch, and The Wardrobe*

. . . so at the wardrobe she stretched
her hands into the thick
of fluffed fur,
and buried her face
in its endless layers,
where warmth hung
and she believed
in the snug
of deep-timbered
darkness,
every limb,
breathing
the songs
of wooded worlds

while at this wood desk I reach
for what is hung
above what I pen,
a lily
painted
in oyster white
wrapping me in limb,

a robe of petals
unfurling
its golden heart
within the whimsy
of grassland wind

beneath the same skies

trusting light
to throw wide
today's leaves

with tomorrow's
then . . .

Marginals

Faith floats
in margins;
ink-stems
coil along
the brink
of words
rippling
across
a page,
hope jots
the shore's
pearly foam
bound before
a scarlet edge
of the loose leaf—
yet our emergents
ride the rolling swells
of sentences, their words
wafting along banks of belief
shallow, rooted in creases of lichened gravel
gathered between land and sea, beneath curled waves of
of some vast truth—   their beauty   still emerging   to bloom.

Months

This month shall be for you the beginning of months. Exodus 12:2

Mercy named the months
for we could not swallow
a minute's luster—
the perpetual,
witnessed pale,
tempered in part
across an hour—
so we might savor
goodness,
its power,
that saturates
our years,
its centuries—
their millenia.

He wrapped us in time,
to sip at its table—
for if we awoke to
to infinite feasts of
memories,
gorged destinies,
their blue moons—
our bloated,
liquid bodies
and engulfed eyes,
would erupt

(from flickering
disbelief)
into drops of
stars spanning
the never-ending
skies.

So bits of seconds
and seasons
are bound—
then dispensed,
delicately,
into a
vanilla scent,
a quiet kiss,
an icicle's drip,
a morning mist—
hemming
time's intent—
its dimness
and its
brilliance.

Raindrop Stories

Every raindrop
bears a story
incubated—

moss blankets hug
timid tears
loosed in silence

beads glide
like terns, brushing
stone-stillness

drizzle buffs
the skins of branches,
and tickles

the plump drips
to crack crisp
the sleepy leaves

tossed in ripples
above dancing rivers
and blooming heaves—

these opened wombs
shoot droplets skyward,
as liquid offspring

bursting heavenward
in love-lept offering
to pregnant clouds

who birth the sodden—
when the drama of dew
awaits the opus
of falling.

Aged

> *But you have kept the good wine until now.* JOHN 2:10

It is taking years for the
furrowed brow of *this can't be*,
to ease into
its full-bodied *now*,
the marvel of *how*

can this be,
when either and or,
twist side to side
for what is just,
for that turn right,

those slow sips
from the dregs
of reason,
when truth heartens
the fermented season—

before life's mercy
spews from the left

and the weight
of my head
spins dizzy round
by what is found

in the *somehow*—
when far is near,
first is last,
fire is cloud,
god is man;

before it all began
and mysteries, like me,
ask to age,

to mature the *now*—

drunk from the barrel
of a wondrous
how.

A Memory

A pleasure is fully grown only when it is remembered. C.S. LEWIS

Nearly numb, it flanks
my mortal tent

and warms
by burning embers

thaws and bends

into recall,
slow-roast melted

and stick-stabbed,
it hangs suspended

near flames
that singe it formless,

a golden bruise
toasted crisp—

till squeezed
between truths

in cream-cracked
confection,

its hidden heart
of sweet redemption,

is licked from lips
and taste is tendered—

and with fondness,
fresh-remembered.

Until Seeing

Pointillism

a duplex

This day feels like a canvas of points,
the soft stipplings of lonely color—

a dawn of dot-to-dots in soft stipplings
of rose that freckle into shy sky-blush

or oak leaf freckles speckled in minted
greens, fanned on the winds I breathe

when I breathe in the pastel hours,
though I know the chill of a blue drip

across the linen, when my blues drip
dappled tears that streak skies in whites

until vistas burst in the whites of my eyes
when I step back and forget each hue

for the whole, each hue's speckled light—
and my day nears a canvas of points.

It may not be an exodus, but what if . . .

on Tuesday's date with socks and sheets and pains,
its musts and mounds of duty-filling daze . . .
she saw her same ole dryer *light in flames*,
what seemed a box of steel broke into blaze!

And if she'd mocked its cheap utility,
til from a fire the glowing dryer *spoke*—
would blasted burn send her to bended knee
within a clouded voice of holy smoke?

Would then she see herself on sacred ground,
and every concrete labor stained as hallow;
if humdrum is what spins this world around
and mystery will find her wearied shadow?

Then how could Wednesday still remain so slight
when what is dull and dry might still blaze bright?

The Angel

Mark 6:52

My tire glazed an ice patch,
spun across the turnpike
and plunged into a gulch of snow
in the lonely hours of the night—

until a lemon plastic jumpsuit waved
in my window—a bald man
wearing citrus, holding chains.

Later, he was an angel—
but then I only believed in
the yellow suit,
in cold coincidence,
in kneeling on Sunday,
and recited prayer—
so I laughed.

Days passed and my young,
spit-filled eyes glimpsed
trees walking,
vats of wine water,
a stray whale,
a wet fleece—
such sundry specters.

Then after years of beholding
the sky-loosed bread,
fat fish-full nets,
water-clogged rocks,
divine winds—
the clouds uncovered
that evening's apparitions,
the moonlit head,
silvery links,
the golden suit

So that sacred storms
unchained my eyes
to feast on manna
and memory
and marvel—
and I could see
and know
what He meant
by the loaves.

The Advent of Hindsight

> *...not having received the things promised, but having seen them and greeted them from afar.* HEBREWS 11:13

The candle burns
in why's advent

when why-bloated
clouds puff and dry

and only tears
wet stills of windows

as we look back
at the relentless road

each gritty
and lopsided step

that sought to summon
a soak with its dance

or stumble on some
slighted spring

when our parched awaits
a watering

the cataract
to drench all doubt—

so we put up trees,
hang our wreaths

sing the carols,
prepare our feasts

and listen
for the tolls of thunder

before what's passed
and what's next

meet under
berried mistletoe

beneath the bath
of sworn Light—

before we awaken
to divine

that promise is hindsight.

Next Year, Plant Roses

Will my forgiveness succumb
to the first frost—
like an annual sown
in glistening spring,
the blush of pink
and green
leave-fold
gloating
its growth
with a bask
in its own
beauty blown
at the garden corner

until the days shorten
with each front,
banes bend
the chilled buds,
then shrivel,
the dry heart
transpiring
in winds
of Fall's
dogged voice

warning it to bloom
only once

so it rolls
its petaled pique
round itself
and wilts

mummified
by the merciless
cold.

Scenic Overlook

It is miles before we pull over—
the curling roads cart our cramped bodies
to where our world thinks we should go
and we peer through the familiar frame
of the windshield at the gray pavement
winding up the pass; we sit restless

behind glass, missing all of the signs:
the refrain of mountain river-song,
a redtail mounting the aqua sky,
the golden regattas of aspens
flapping high over sea green valleys,
all waving, *Over here! Come and see!*

For us, detours are a squandering,
of restraint, a kiss with a missed
turn, a brush with a jam of strangers,
a rock to crack our taut windows,
frighten our maps free from their folds
and take our fixed eyes from routine roads

that train our leadened hungers and hearts
to slow for the rudimentary,
the plea of some mass-formed image:
two words and a simple stick figure
peering through a tiny telescope—
Scenic Overlook, it says to us

if only we could hear it, begging
us to roll down our tinted windows,
to blow free the hair from bleary eyes,
invite us to waltz with rolling hills,
wave back to the pines and hum our hymns
with the steady rhythms of rivers—

but the board just offers an exit:
to park and walk toward the cemented
edge, the concrete for stiff travelers,
for those who ignore behind the glass,
the unraveling beauty they pass through
the panes of the safe and forgotten.

A New Moon

> *The comfortable people want only wax moon faces, poreless, hairless, and expressionless.* RAY BRADBURY

Before, she only slept eastward

so dawn's foreseen light flickered
through the leaves freckling her face

and what lay behind, the past,
and all that followed, lolled

suspended in the hollow of nightfall—
despite the day, shadows hid

her open pores, cell-bound graves
unsteamed, clogged in oily stores

of rotated hours, her joy buried
in the waning— until one day's dusk

the new moon's gentle ghost
whispered in evening's clouds,

its breath dampening her skin,
loosening the fissures of dried flakes

in a wash of warmth—

and she rolled over, smoothing her cratered bed
and faced the phases of all that followed

from the east

and the west.

Lake Day

We splash the clouds,
      slapping what floats
on our wet playground,
      laughing in the mirrors
of liquid magic—

we jump in the galactic
      from docks, where light
streaks the surface in a glitter
      of daystars

and we drift
      over mountains on rafts,
peering beneath
      for creatures, for secrets;

our ripened bodies lunge
      across the swells,
and cedar-chains blanket
      the shoreline as we walk
their water ghosts—

we spring for the up-side down,
      what we kick with our feet
and spit through the puckered lips
      of all our pretend,

swashing such fancies
        that glow in the day's glint,
bolstered by waves
        that slide through fingertips—

then buoyed by the day's end,
        we spring from the depth-less,
leap to dry ground,
        and wrap our bright bodies
in towels, looking to the sky

up . . . into the oak tree
        looming over our frames,
its weathered arms spreading
        its breadth, its age,
its sense, across our banks—

and through its limbs we spy
        the same billows,
what our fists sloshed,
        what we tossed
in the child-mirrors of our shallows

and we collapse like shadows
        groundward, to the rooted,
coughing up candor of youth,
        and puffed perceptions—

only to search the waters
        silly and shy—
shivering in the gaze
        of sun-dried reflections.

A Mast Year

Pecans fell like rain
that fall, lime-gold husks
blanketed blades

of green, fracturing
shadows of drupe-
laden boughs

as children cached
shells in giant shirts
and shucks cracked

the cries of jubilee
beneath tiny feet—
what bounty!

when baths of lingering
spring rinse the rise
of a flowering

and tunneled bridges
of fungal share
their alms

whispered
as wind-giggled gifts
of sugar breath

while skins
laugh sheds
of fruit-showers

and we gather—
in rhythmic romp
to store

all we had forgotten
beneath the beauty
of more.

I try to learn jam band

for Ben

It's that we're unsure
of the fifteen minute song,
such wait between
the leaving
and returning—
we join with the first lyric
the poetic ache
each versed wish
before it gives way
to the meanwhile
the slow slide
to wilderness
the fear of what's wordless—
and yet what we hear
is a beat percussing,
holding the groove
of furied fingers
running across the taut
of threads
some scissored shreds
that spawn
the unleashing of keys
in its wild un-theme
yet somehow in sync
with each plucked string—

before tension builds
and the crowd leans
for the unfold,
the waking from a dream,
a thump
across the threshold—

and instead we're tuned,
to a story un-told,
when parts are lost
beneath chords
to song-raveled soul
and what's major
becomes minor
as we succumb
to the jam

and find what matters
is simply
the dance.

To Lose My Voice

It once bounced across bathtub bubbles,
and baby cries drowned beneath echoes
from my shallow well of motherhood.

Where from my quiet lap she'd croon
for one more story, and our utters chimed
to the honeyed ties of harmony.

Too soon the outros of childhood played,
words ricocheted in the crevices
of crooked brows and cords drew curtains.

My fluctuating folds danced in front
of closed doors, giving way to whisper,
air strumming tendons soft to a sigh.

For a daughter will heed more voices
and what is wrenched slows to its wonted
hibernation—*to voice as listening—*

for the soundless; for the breath of skies
to still sing through our bubbled broken,
reminding us both . . . we are spoken.

Thresholds

for Lauren

You perch at a common threshold,
Eye's gleam in doorways' laughter,
And wave goodbye to ticking time.
I am unable to find lost words
Spilled over the milk at our table
Or heaped in mom-love letters.

I recall, smiling, how you learned letters;
Those years waited at day's threshold,
Hours spent at the school table,
Chasing backyard butterflies in laughter,
Cuddled on the couch holding words,
Cherished moments of little time.

You grew wings with the flying time.
Gone were handwritten letters,
Swallowed with the raw words,
As you teetered at childhood's threshold,
Joining in the uneasy laughter
Of suspicions at the lunch table.

Later kneeling at the Sabbath table,
Someone prayed for us this time,
Begetting our Sunday lunch laughter,
Then remembered in the letters,
Knowing the Spirit spans the threshold,
And prayers are more than words.

Your joy gifts me tender words.
We sip coffee at the shared table
And consider the opening threshold:
Fly rainbows and travel the time;
Never lament writing me letters;
Fill your hours with long laughter.

Tears will never drown laughter.
Days will become more than words.
Yes, you will always have my letters.
And your chair will rest at our table
Til we feast again, in time.
I hear silence at the threshold.

Yes, years waited at day's threshold,
And words piled into time's letters,
Leaving laughter's echo at the table.

Until Following

Dusted

May you be covered in the dust of your rabbi . . .
FIRST CENTURY JEWISH BLESSING

so sifted in the soot of his sandals
that you're close enough to talc your trailing
feet in the whirling specks of each step's tread,
wrapping your tarry in a russet mist,
the powdery cloud in which you stumble
blind, learning to abide the murkiness
of his spurned shadow on an untraveled
byway, a prepared high-way . . . when it is dust

that forms you, and you are free to follow,
to catch the fallen crumbs, to breathe the rot
of lepers, to rub the muddied sorrow,
to live as his—to carry your own cross
in wake of his rivened flesh, so throwing
aside your sandals and kicking up dust.

I share the shadow

I share the shadow
of a leper—

side by side
in grotesque guise
we grovel
after the sun;

the pale splotches
of scarred skins
and curled limbs
hide in the umbra
of our numb;

darkness reddens
our flush
into broken blush,
no one sees
nor would touch

our ghostly soul—

until . . . the shadow cast
and plaguing past
graze the shade
of a forgotten hour

when love was lifted
with mending power
and skinned,
hammered

crossed
on that eclipsed plateau—

where we share
in the dusk
of its winged shadow.

Lamenting Sackcloth

I ransacked the attic,
rummaging
through bygone
bags and days,
what felt musty
in filth long-frayed—

and unearthed
this burlap habit,
hemmed, fashioned,
suited for sabbath

but so massive,
so I groped tight
its wooded grit

and with dull blade,
I fabricated
a flaxed fit,

some suitable dress—

(heartless, I confess)

and it just fell,
with hope impaled—

so I wear
the grief
of not grieving,

guilt unwailed—

now my coarse heart
hangs heavy
with what
won't rend—
baggy and callous
beneath its own skin.

Melting Point

He tarried at the hem
of it all melting

back hunched beneath
the weight of his wondering

if those leavened flakes
would forever be falling—

he sits fixed at the slit
eyes in their twitching

broken body bent
in the ballast of waiting

limp muscles drained
in the dry desert dawning

til awakened again
by the spill of a breading

after the midnight sweats
still soaked his bedding—

his silence listened
to drops of lost blessing

drowned by the thuds
of his own thoughts grumbling

of hands that tired
in the gleaning and rubbing;

but as morning retreated
with another sun's waxing

his stomached need
stretched to the opening

and with rainy eyes
he gaped again gazing

at the provision gifted,
yet grieved by the waning—

for doubt is still fed
during a midday melting

though goodness is given
each plentiful morning.

Leaving the Suburbs

It's when your faith
laps the cul-de-sac,
looping the chain
of locked doors,
dizzied by hemmed
lots of bricked
humdrum
and stenciled
limbs—
what trims
the land
scapes
of your plots

(again
and again
around
the same
bend)

that you long to veer
off the impasse,
to swerve
unpaved
and gape
at some place

of jungled,
rutted romp
that refuses
another round
of the same bend

but wills

a risky whirl . . .

before the dead end.

Dawnsongs

A rooster crows
and I cower
behind the memories
of my own deceit.

For I, too, invite
trios of crows—
the bird's hackle swells,
stretches long
to shake me
and blood-red combs
tilt like hell's flames
toward the heavens.

Yet the dreaded cries,
these avian warnings,
sound an awakening,
a reminder of refuge,
of the morn and
its mercies—

Now on the steeple
the vane of
the cock's tail twirls,
catches the dove-breaths,
foretells the winds—

that seasons spin,
and birdsongs
may herald
guilt and grace
in the same breath.

Threadbare

a few frail syllables flap
in the fraying of phrases—

> *thy*, the mended fabric
> of prayer, dangles

before *come*, a tendril tattered
in the waiting of what?

> His *will*, that elastic word,
> its pull, back and forth

when *done* feels bound
but instead unravels

> into the mere babble of *give*;
> spit-spun, and hung

before *bread*, what's risen,
then torn, soft in the shred

> and unknotted *for-give* . . .
> sin-seams unlace

and lament is bound
to *lead*, is baste,

    until my voice cries *deliver,*
    from what's now darned

to that final *forever*
where I hold on—

    so stitches,
    stuttered,

    unthreaded,

    leave me tethered

    in torn-up prayer.

Edges

> *Do not reap to the very edges of your field . . . Leave them for the poor and the foreigner.* LEVITICUS 19:9-10

I scrub again at the kitchen sink—
a steady stream spilling
into my parched hands
and frustrated dreams
while I sputter
tepid pleas
that berth on
the basin's edge—

words risen from my own deep—
from the grocery lane
or waiting game;
petitions piled
like laundry,
sighed in anxious nights,
mumbled between bites,
churned cheap
from the church pew—

maybe He will consider
the edges
of this filthy sink,
garnering drops
of my disregard,

(like exhaust, spewn,
hail mary's and hallelujahs
in one breath,
leftovers landing
on fringes
for the broken,
for myself)

and scatter
the spittled seeds
of my sore needs,

crumbs wanting

to leave the brink,
this sink

and inch toward
the heart
of the harvest.

Amen Is a Watershed

> HEIDELBERG CATECHISM QUESTION #129: *"Amen" signifies, it shall truly and certainly be: for my prayer is more assuredly heard of God, than I feel in my heart that I desire these things of him.*

I prayed to love my enemy
mumbling the amen—
dank words puddling
again, in the parking lot
of a paved soul
where reservoirs
of silt pile
and rise
evading
a bathe
in mercy's
mending rill—

until the steep
lean of love's
long hill
trickles
my petition
into running
spill,

the currents
of their assured
end

to the infinite oceans
of a heard
amen.

A Box to Go with You

for Nathan

> . . . *talk of them when you sit in your house, and when you walk by the way, when you lie down, and when you rise* . . . DEUTERONOMY 6:7

So what has filled this old phylactery?
What will you remember rested between
the frames of your mother's rueful forehead,
photos, doors, and dreams? Have I left unvoiced
all that was boxed inside this shy heart, trussed,
what should have been hallowed from our rooftop . . .
Love the Lord your God, penned on fragile skin?
Oh, that what I felt, the want of my words
might still speak for Him—all my *I love yous,*
unrolled with what should be taut, will they wrap
around the good that will pass and later
unfold with those papered promises sought—
my words wound around all of your within
so that my love lives as reminder of Him.

Drafting

We may find our selves
in the slipstream

>lifted in the wake
of the fold's faith

and pain—
when it's not our race

>but we share
its shadow-drag

and cling to wings
shred in gales

>lean in the lane's
downstream

glide the tide
of dove-breaths

>that whisk the body
in a long tack

through grief's strain
and stained glass—

    til belief buoys upon
    willowed whispers

and we are weightless before
the fogged shore.

Postlude

the last note of
the old organ lingers
holding on to
its own, long history—

the rooms fills with
that heavy,
hanging
postlude pause—

and the humble
murmurs of men
pour into
the empty space—

pasteurized pleasantries
float the balcony—
down the aisle—
through the stairwell—
to the sidewalk.

(I listen, yearning for the quiet)

yet the saturated sounds,
the simple harmonies of
family chatter,
suddenly surprise—

synchronize—

whisking with the hour's
moist notes
and wisdom-wet words,
softening my spirit—

stirring curdled anxieties
and clotted choler
and lumped regrets
into batters of belief—

the music of the murmur
melds with Sabbath melody;
and its truth solidifies—
incarnating into
a full feast.

Laughter Can Echo to Monday

Laughter can echo
to Monday,
the wave born from
Sabbath liturgy,
resounding in song,
then fed with
bread broken
at the table of love.

Peals reach across
the tired carpet,
cheerful chortles,
girlish giggles
ripple past
unmade memories
of tomorrow
and its thistles.

Wellsprings of glee
glimmer across
the room into dusky
Sunday dreams,
past the midnight hours
of dread and silence,
like a hymn,
giving hope
to Monday's unknown.

Matins

for Greg

I'm not always there, but this morning when I closed the door and knelt cross-legged on the carpet beneath our bedroom window, awaiting the small patch of light that breaks on the pine, hoping to find in the darkness some flicker inside, I shut my eyes and pled for Him to near, to suspend the silence parading my ear . . . until the door cracked open, and you tiptoed shy behind, stirring the stillness when you passed by, and a breeze stirred and brushed the back of my neck, embodying all that I begged . . . so with long breath I bowed my chest and head, tucking myself into the cleft of our bed—for I could not see your face, but knew you well in the soft place on which we tread, where I felt your hand with His cover mine, where we are found, hand under hand under Hand . . . so I bent low and lay hushed on that holy ground.

Still Life

Psalm 131

she paints a still life—

its bowl of golden apples
waiting whole

on time's table, in flit
and flicker of candle

flaming through the pane
of a dimmed window;

a round loaf risen
beneath the days broken

beside a scarlet rose
limp, woven;

and lone daisy, a vase's grazing
of death and life, wound;

while at the table's rim
two seashells sound

brushed thin with the sands
of soft shore

and at its core, a pale skull,
the careful sockets

reminiscent of that gray
Golgotha, what is ours . . .

so she paints in stilled light
beneath the divine life

rising above shadows
of the illumined table

of still beauty

and quiet soul.

Until Rising

Grandfather's Visit

a psalm of ascent

Our Pops still missed the door to his guestroom;
he walked his chocolate pie to the garage
chanting, *this is my house, I know my way.*

We witnessed his own wits and ways unhinge
from today, as the doors swung too wide,
turning handles to the past or imagined.

He begged to invite his dad for supper
and paced along our windows, hailing
the unknown neighbors with backdoor hellos.

Hundreds of boxed memories were tossed,
flashbacks from Asian trenches were spilled
with sentence fragments and indefinites.

We wanted to plug these portals, slow-close corks
to keep thieves from what's lucid, what seduces
a broken mind through its threshold.

But age shut the door on the rational,
and words twisted into confusing knots
that we struggled to loosen and unlace

Until that third day . . . when our sabbath doors
flung open to a world unclocked and staid;
where the spirit unlocks our penned-up place

And those first notes of the well-worn hymn
were love-transposed, so our Pops' voice
rose—above the time, unlatching to find

the door of ushered words sung true—
where psalms approach the waiting gates
of then and now and what will be new.

At the Park's Cancer Bell

She heaved its raveled rope
with her right fist
as chords
of the opera
resounded
on the phone
in her left,
the thin boughs
of both arms
lifting to conduct
their harsh
polyphony

a long fermata . . .

echoing from a bell
hung within willows,
where life suspended
in seasons of leaves
and she swayed
with the trees
to its toll

blowing
from the aria
of her hands

the solo

belted across
star-crossed stages

of wait,
keep walking,
listen to the bird's bel
canto trilled
to the lilt

of tears
trickling staccato

down her limbs,
moistening

the harmony
of all she held

within what was
her right
and her left.

The Vanishing Point

I stood in a dusty gallery
with an aged landscape—

framed with
foreground trees
bent inward
beneath blue,
the horizon's steep
sky enfolded over
burgeoning branches,
in view

distant figures,
a lifeless horse,
blurred—
the artist's lines
swallowing,
their end,
a destiny,
inferred

and I wondered—
at its two dimensions,
man-mixed colors,

the curtain of trees
of knowledge,
of life,
framing the scene,
forging skyline—

that what is formed
with words, and dust
could converge
with what's imagined,
a promised line
between earth
and heaven—

so that my eyes
have nowhere else
to go—
but to that point,
invisible, but known,
the place where
storied trees
are fully grown.

The Drift

> *Give me my scallop shell of quiet* . . . WALTER RALEIGH

Give me my scallop shell
of quiet

in the bottomed bed
of forsaken seas

between the ribs
of oceaned will

the slow-flow
of pilgrim swell—

do not shuck me
from hallowed grooves

of the salted, swept
through my rift—

when currents shift
let me float

this fan of fluted favor
in wine-drunk drift,

rested in the rippling
of aged rings,

their dawn-tinge dusk
draping the bend—

until my unhinged husk
pipes its bubbled urge

and tides tarry, then surge
to shell-grave shore—

and cracked wreckage
listens for the lure

of trumpets—escorting
whispers of pearl.

Windthrow

We paddle our grief
past

and sigh at the savagery
of tree toppling

the uproot
from primordial soil

cloud blather,
breeze brush

perpetual rinse
and reflection

rings can't count
such loss—

when a ruthless gust
razes the oak's boast

in its cradled nest,
uttered leaves, branch-dance

the peak of gallantry
rend in the unearthing

of lattice, when
brokenness mines

a root labyrinthe
uncloaked

as miry temple
whose beneath

teems with the living,
the vulnerable—

when it forgets
its reflection

in its plunge
to humble sanctum—

as resurrected umbra,
life for the fallen.

Ms. Lela

Isaiah 61:3

For years she lived
without legs, laden
by the two flush snags
broken beneath
her teeming heart
which fought to lift
the blinds of each day
with rinded arm,
stretching her tired trunk
toward light,
where thirsty skin
could sip the dews
dripped from
another mercy's dawn—

until dusk welcomed
her body to rest,
and shaded the oak
that she now knows—
its garden-ground
laving stumps
in celestial rivers
where the forgotten
parch of roots long-lap,
lacing mended limbs
in syrup of endless sap.

Espalier

I do not imagine
a trellised heaven,

an espalier of
flush fruit

sheared, manicured,
pruned

or woven
into twisted train,

against flanked stone
or flattened plane,

an ordering of drupes,
their crop confined

to measure groove
or knotted line—

instead our vines
will bound the hills

unlaced loosely where
fruit wills

weaving through orchards
knitting the grasses

their juices spilling
into river splashes.

Unraveling

When we let go of ours horizons—the ropes we tug from east to west
                the cords riving
    the fall   and rise
        of our day's sun—

      what we keep taut in the panorama
    of left   and right,
    the line of sky   over which sight
        will never peek

      when our safe lines
      roll into skeins—
   to unframe a day's familiar
       fabric

our grips loosening   the thin thread
            that splits
  our earth   from our heaven—

       joy unwinds

   and the point of our vanishing
      loses its sting

   in the seamless merge
     with all
     unseen.

A Final Volta

I prayed my final poem to be dreamt—
with revelations of symbolic art,
apocalyptic mines I've prophesied
in early verse, the final pearls bestowed
to heirs, the *last things* bared in a poet's
uncovering, before new genesis
awaits its opening, and words distill
to wisdom—yet, as images alight
on pages, stretching toward the end of lines,
I hope my pen still turns to orbit round
to *first things*; what resounds the beginning,
when void was filled with answer, dawning light
by breath, the seen, when Word was with—and was—
giving birth to poem, to dream—to final word.

www.ingramcontent.com/pod-product-compliance
Lightning Source LLC
Chambersburg PA
CBHW071730040426
42446CB00011B/2300